GRAPHIC HISTORY

THE VOYAGE OF THE

Mayflower

by Allison Lassieur

illustrated by Peter McDonnell

Consultant:
Walter W. Woodward
Assistant Professor of History
University of Connecticut, Hartford

Capstone

Mankato, Minnesota

Graphic Library is published by Capstone Press,
151 Good Counsel Drive, P.O. Box 669, Mankato, Minnesota 56002.
www.capstonepub.com

Library of Congress Cataloging-in-Publication Data
Lassieur, Allison.
The voyage of the Mayflower / by Allison Lassieur; illustrated by Peter McDonnell.
p. cm.—(Graphic library. Graphic history)
Summary: "In graphic novel format, tells the story of the colonists who traveled to North America in 1620 on the Mayflower, their reasons for coming, and how they started Plymouth Colony"—Provided by publisher.
Includes bibliographical references and index.
ISBN-13: 978-0-7368-4371-3 (hardcover) ISBN-10: 0-7368-4371-X (hardcover)
ISBN-13: 978-0-7368-6211-0 (softcover pbk.) ISBN-10: 0-7368-6211-0 (softcover pbk.)
1. Mayflower (Ship)—Juvenile literature. 2. Pilgrims (New Plymouth Colony)—Juvenile literature. 3. Massachusetts—History—New Plymouth, 1620–1691—Juvenile literature.
I. McDonnell, Peter, ill. II. Title. III. Series.
F68.L37 2006
974.4'8202—dc22 2005008109

Art and Editorial Direction
Jason Knudson and Blake A. Hoena

Designer
Jason Knudson

Editor
Rebecca Glaser

Editor's note: Direct quotations from primary sources are indicated by a yellow background.

Direct quotations appear on the following pages:
Page 7 (both), from *Of Plymouth Plantation* by William Bradford (New York: Alfred Knopf, 1952.)
Page 11, letter from John Robinson to congregation, printed in *Of Plymouth Plantation* by William Bradford (New York: Alfred Knopf, 1952.)
Page 13, letter from Robert Cushman, printed in *Of Plymouth Plantation* by William Bradford (New York: Alfred Knopf, 1952.)
Page 23, from *Of Plymouth Plantation* by William Bradford (New York: Alfred Knopf, 1952.)

Printed in the United States 5889

Table of Contents

CHAPTER 1

Plans for a New Life

England had one official church in the early 1600s. If you didn't belong to the Church of England, you were breaking the law. Some groups were willing to worship secretly and risk arrest to practice their own beliefs. One of these groups was the Separatists. They wanted to follow God's word simply, without the extra rules set by the Church of England.

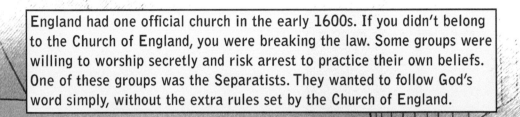

By order of the king, you're under arrest! This church is illegal.

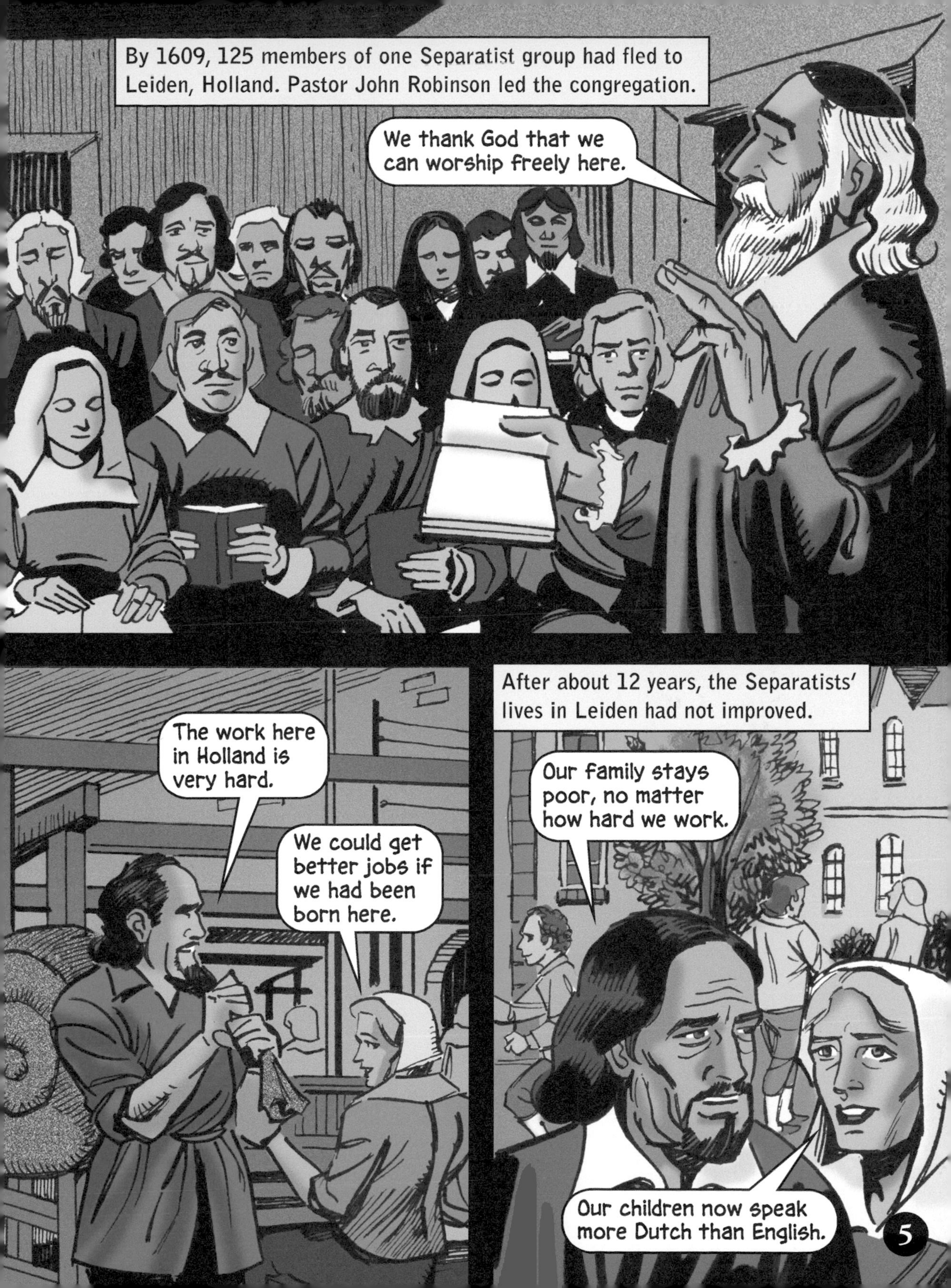
By 1609, 125 members of one Separatist group had fled to Leiden, Holland. Pastor John Robinson led the congregation.
We thank God that we can worship freely here.
The work here in Holland is very hard.
We could get better jobs if we had been born here.
After about 12 years, the Separatists' lives in Leiden had not improved.
Our family stays poor, no matter how hard we work.
Our children now speak more Dutch than English.

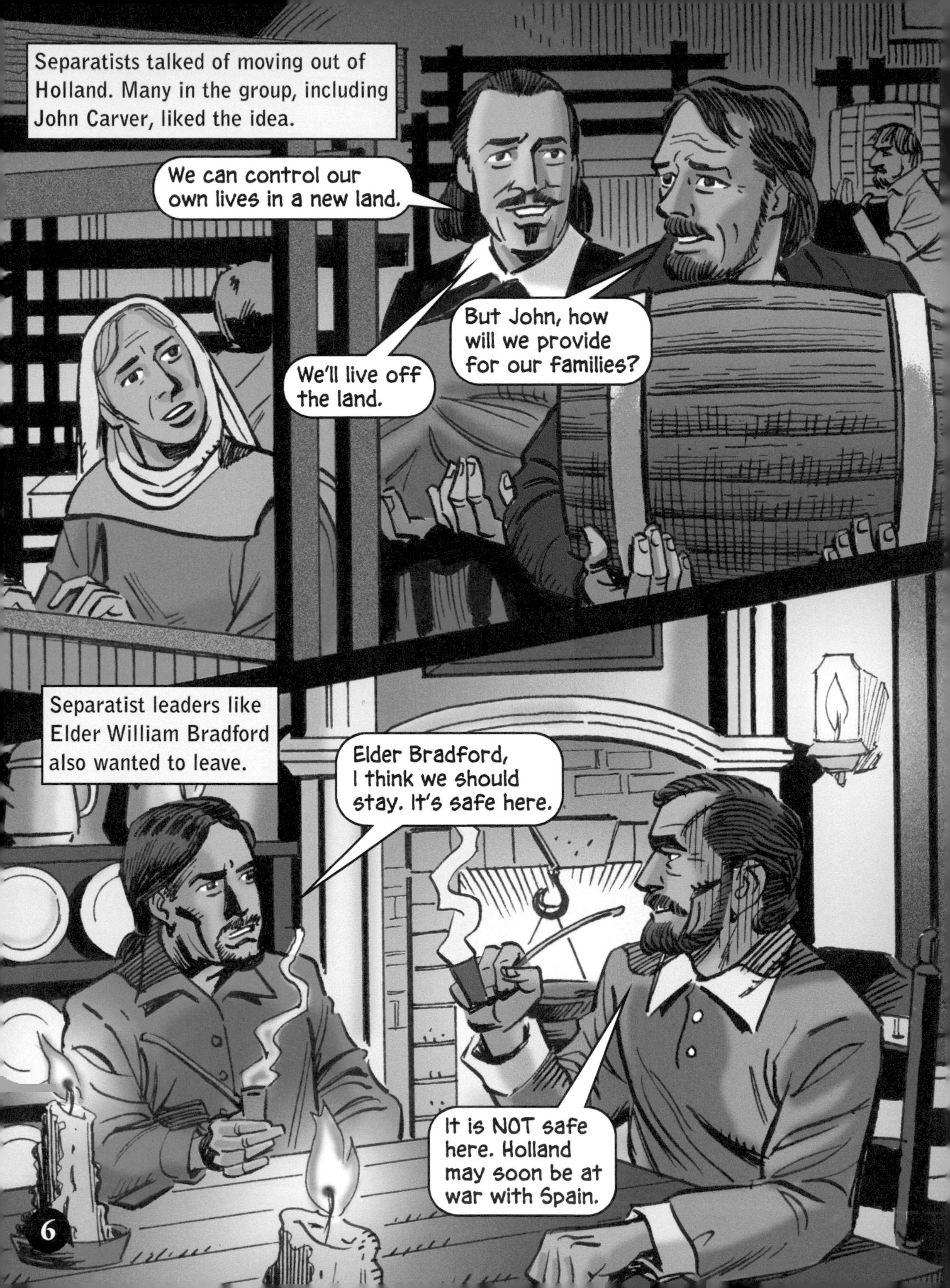
Separatists talked of moving out of Holland. Many in the group, including John Carver, liked the idea.
We can control our own lives in a new land.
But John, how will we provide for our families?
We'll live off the land.
Separatist leaders like Elder William Bradford also wanted to leave.
Elder Bradford, I think we should stay. It's safe here.
It is NOT safe here. Holland may soon be at war with Spain.

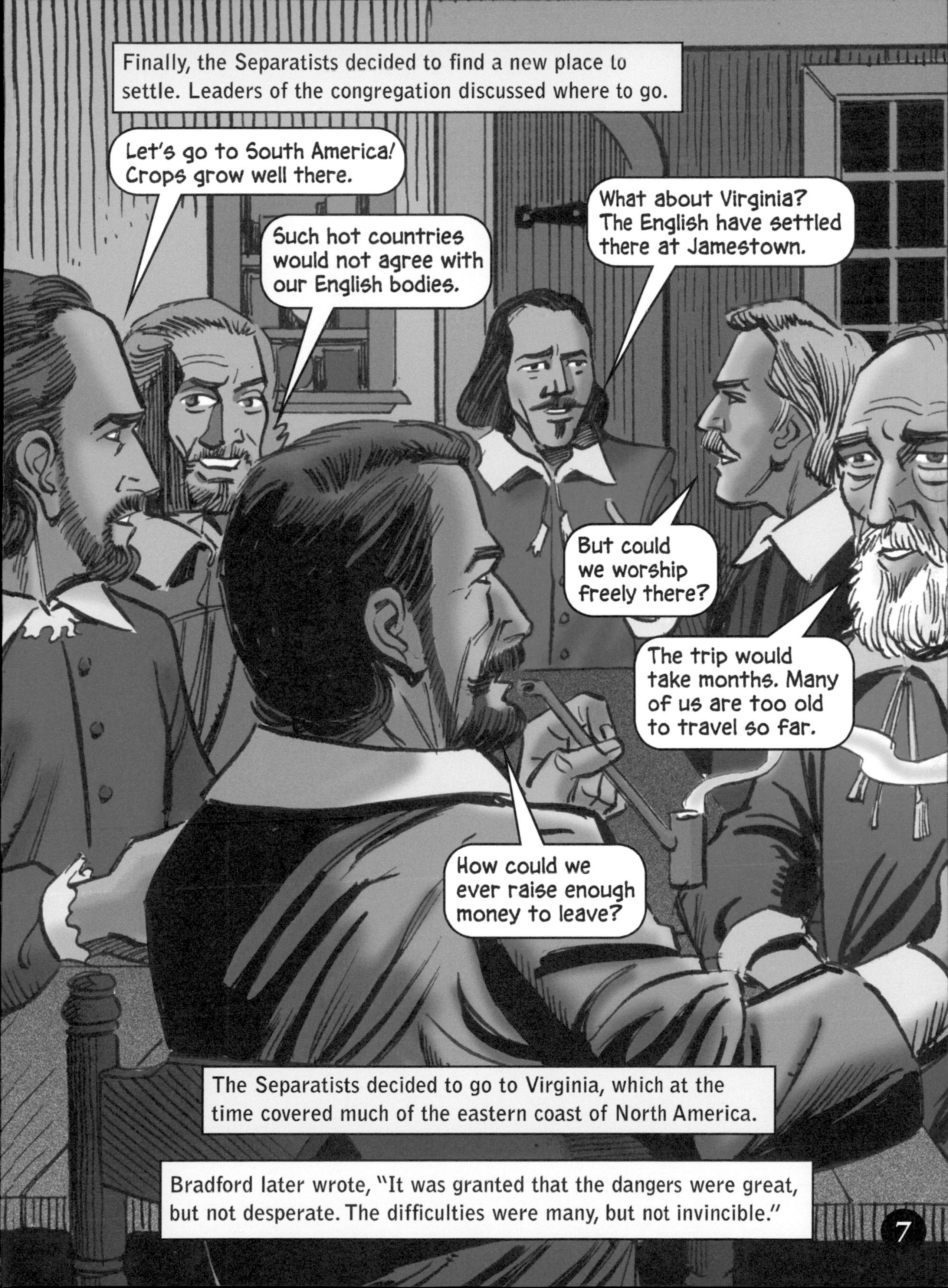

Finally, the Separatists decided to find a new place to settle. Leaders of the congregation discussed where to go.
Let's go to South America! Crops grow well there.
Such hot countries would not agree with our English bodies.
What about Virginia? The English have settled there at Jamestown.
But could we worship freely there?
The trip would take months. Many of us are too old to travel so far.
How could we ever raise enough money to leave?
The Separatists decided to go to Virginia, which at the time covered much of the eastern coast of North America.
Bradford later wrote, "It was granted that the dangers were great, but not desperate. The difficulties were many, but not invincible."

CHAPTER 2

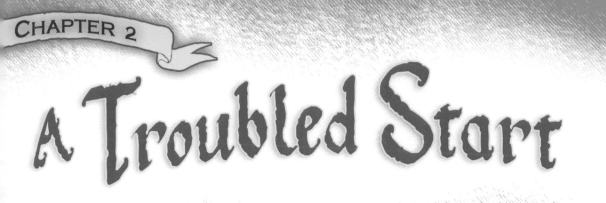

A Troubled Start

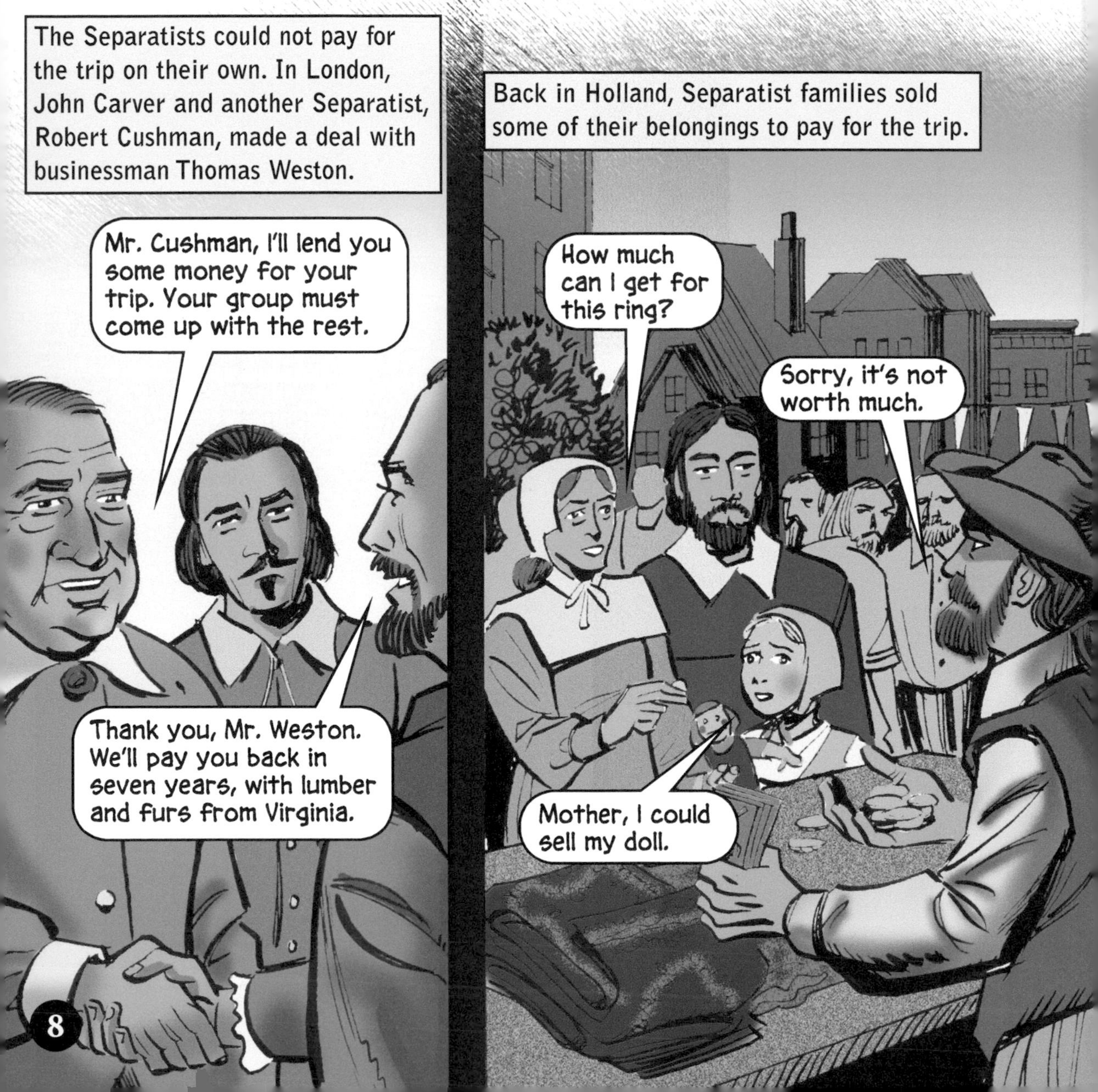

The Separatists could not pay for the trip on their own. In London, John Carver and another Separatist, Robert Cushman, made a deal with businessman Thomas Weston.
Mr. Cushman, I'll lend you some money for your trip. Your group must come up with the rest.
Thank you, Mr. Weston. We'll pay you back in seven years, with lumber and furs from Virginia.
Back in Holland, Separatist families sold some of their belongings to pay for the trip.
How much can I get for this ring?
Sorry, it's not worth much.
Mother, I could sell my doll.

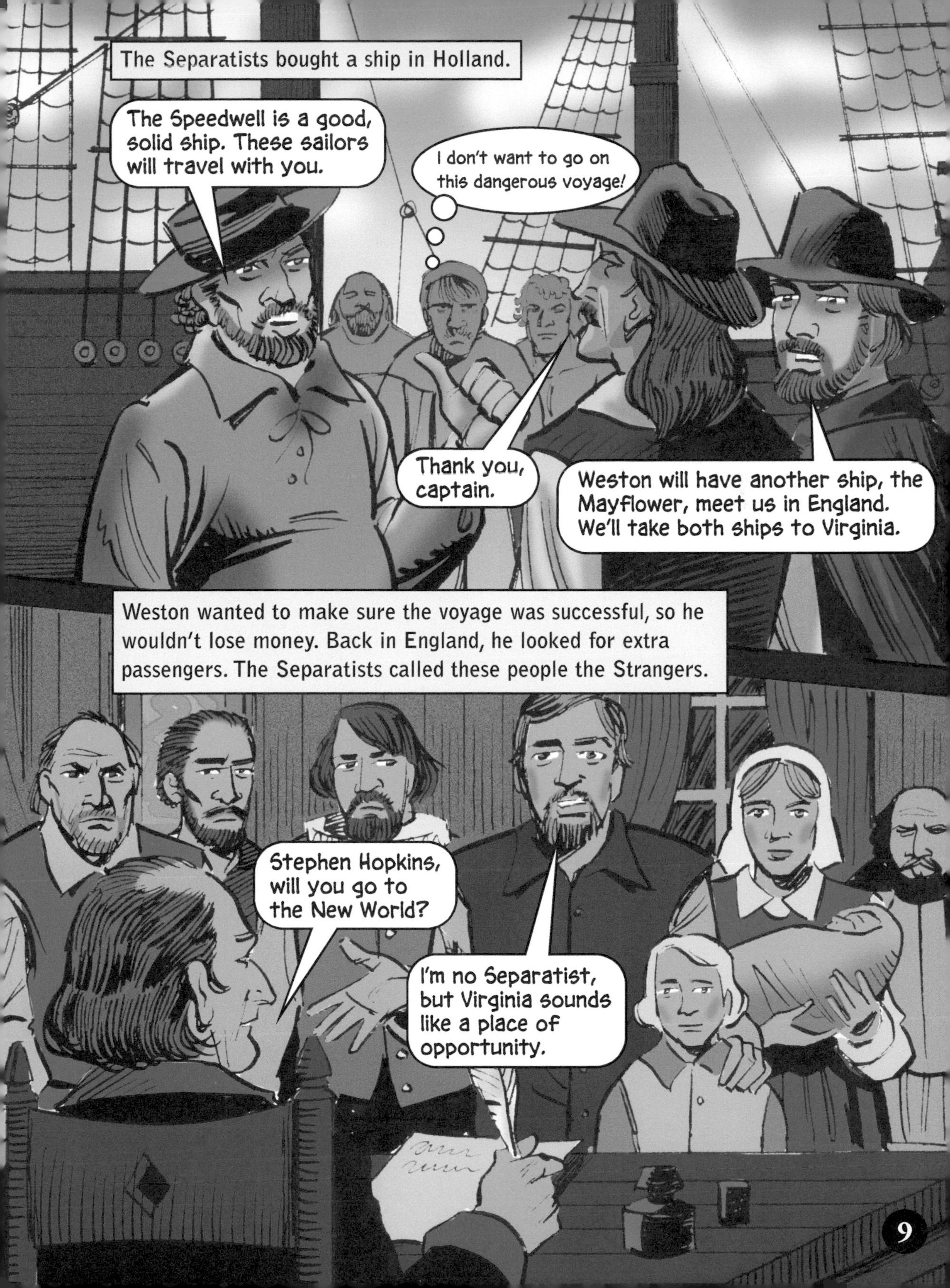
The Separatists bought a ship in Holland.
The Speedwell is a good, solid ship. These sailors will travel with you.
I don't want to go on this dangerous voyage!
Thank you, captain.
Weston will have another ship, the Mayflower, meet us in England. We'll take both ships to Virginia.
Weston wanted to make sure the voyage was successful, so he wouldn't lose money. Back in England, he looked for extra passengers. The Separatists called these people the Strangers.
Stephen Hopkins, will you go to the New World?
I'm no Separatist, but Virginia sounds like a place of opportunity.

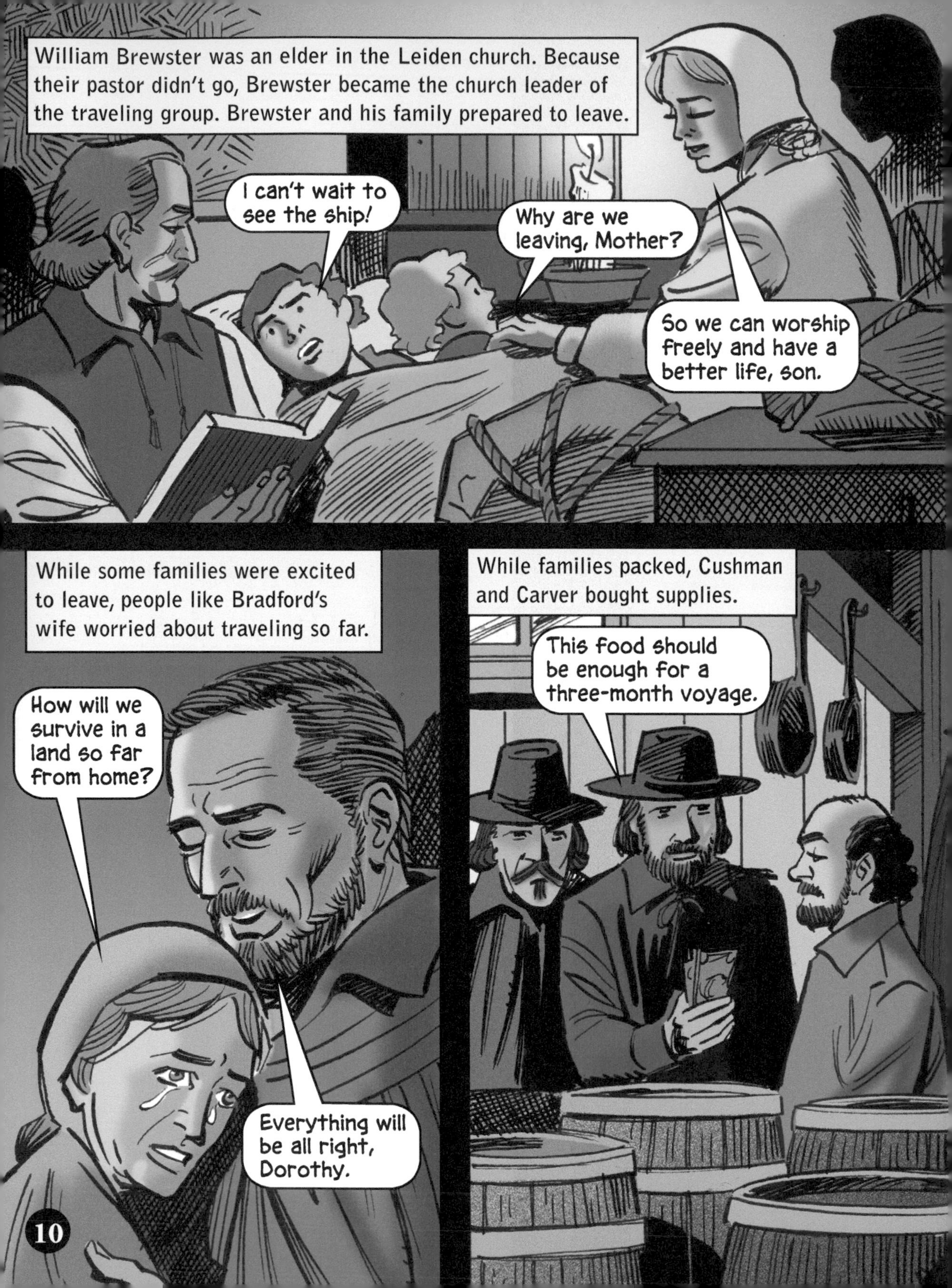
William Brewster was an elder in the Leiden church. Because their pastor didn't go, Brewster became the church leader of the traveling group. Brewster and his family prepared to leave.
I can't wait to see the ship!
Why are we leaving, Mother?
So we can worship freely and have a better life, son.
While some families were excited to leave, people like Bradford's wife worried about traveling so far.
How will we survive in a land so far from home?
Everything will be all right, Dorothy.
While families packed, Cushman and Carver bought supplies.
This food should be enough for a three-month voyage.

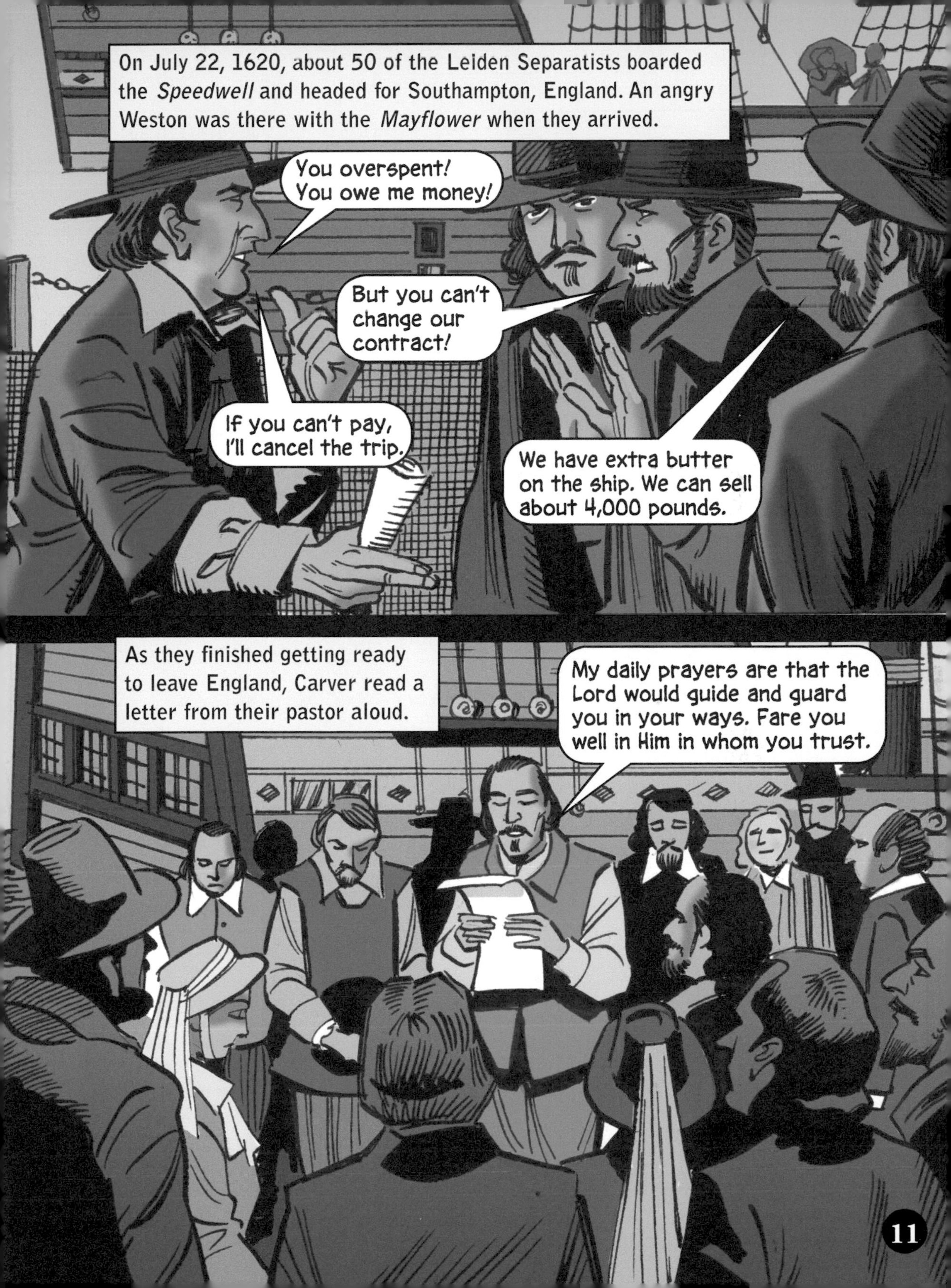

On July 22, 1620, about 50 of the Leiden Separatists boarded the *Speedwell* and headed for Southampton, England. An angry Weston was there with the *Mayflower* when they arrived.
You overspent! You owe me money!
But you can't change our contract!
If you can't pay, I'll cancel the trip.
We have extra butter on the ship. We can sell about 4,000 pounds.
As they finished getting ready to leave England, Carver read a letter from their pastor aloud.
My daily prayers are that the Lord would guide and guard you in your ways. Fare you well in Him in whom you trust.

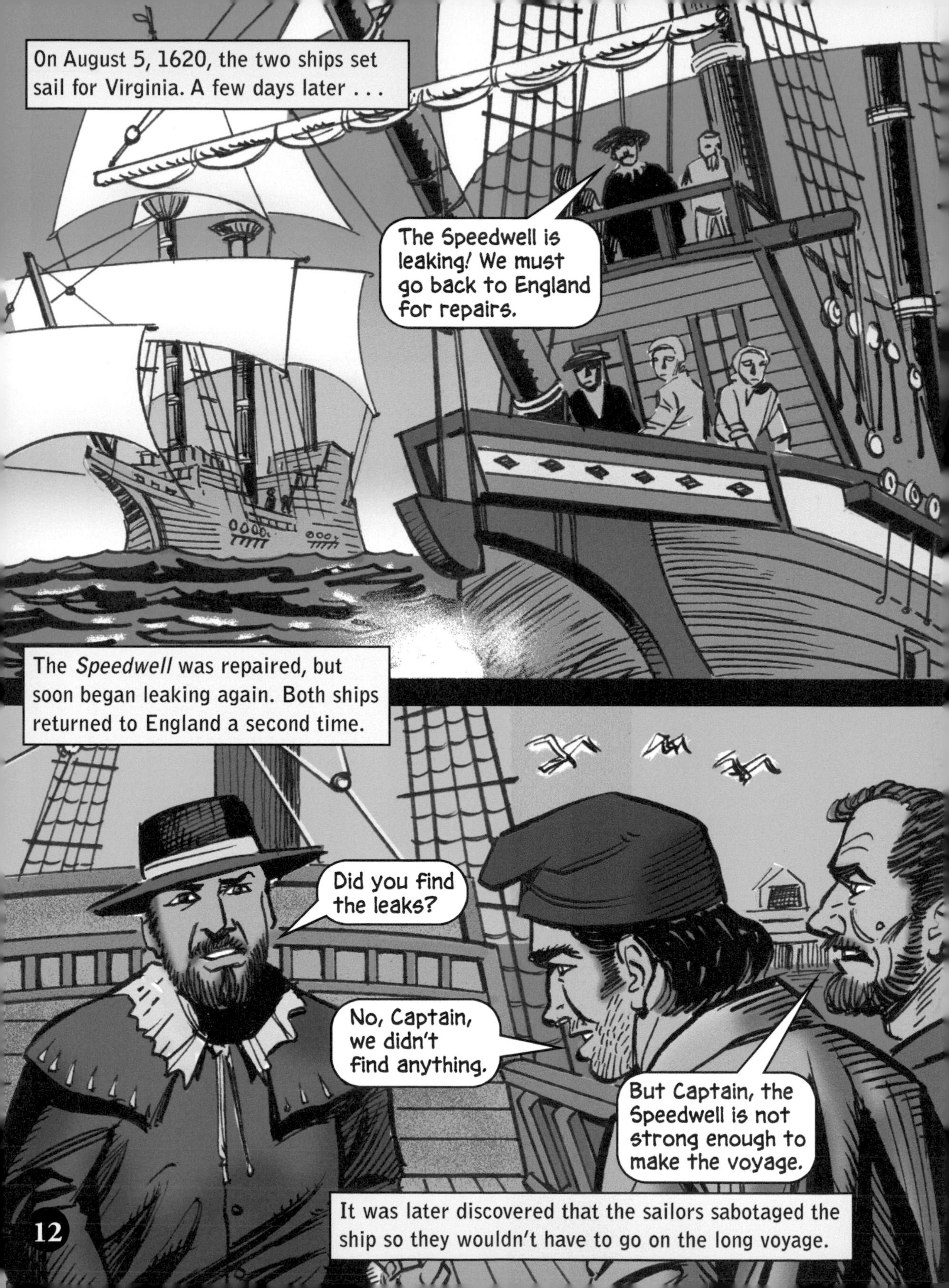
On August 5, 1620, the two ships set sail for Virginia. A few days later . . .
The Speedwell is leaking! We must go back to England for repairs.
The *Speedwell* was repaired, but soon began leaking again. Both ships returned to England a second time.
Did you find the leaks?
No, Captain, we didn't find anything.
But Captain, the Speedwell is not strong enough to make the voyage.
It was later discovered that the sailors sabotaged the ship so they wouldn't have to go on the long voyage.

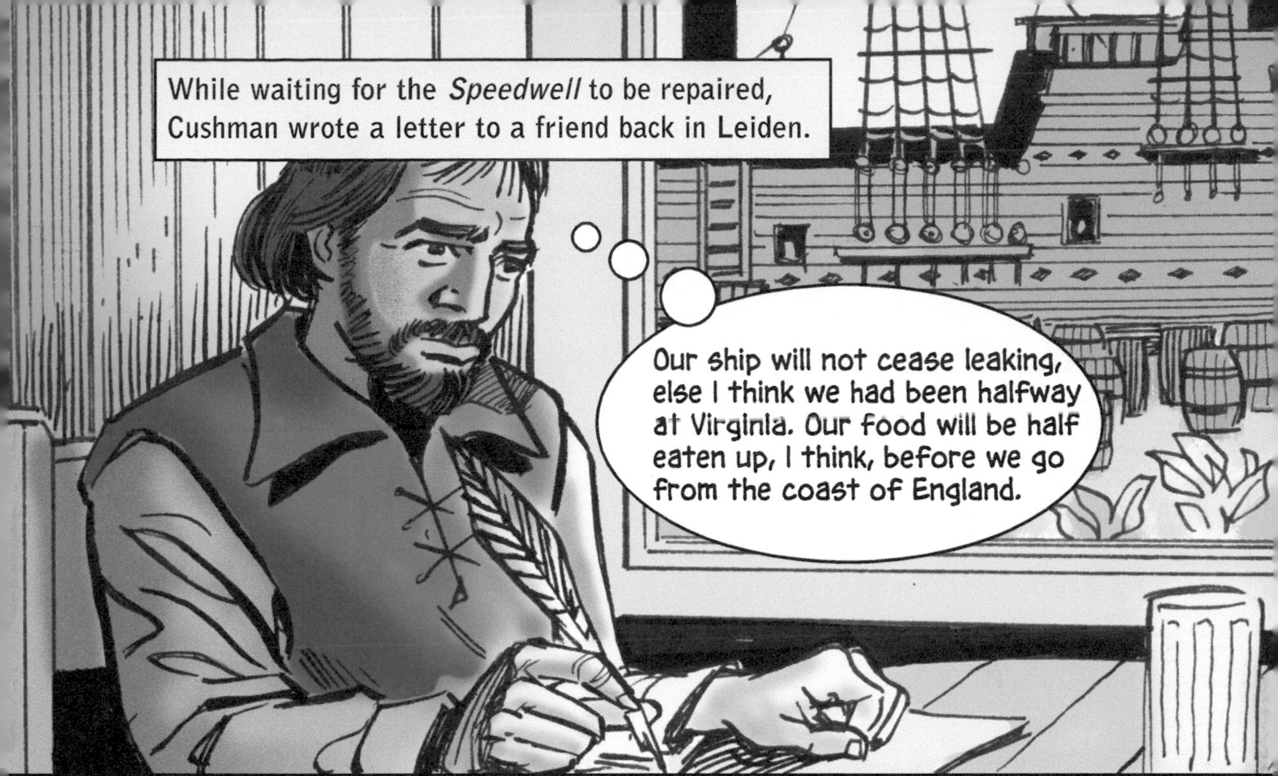
While waiting for the *Speedwell* to be repaired, Cushman wrote a letter to a friend back in Leiden.
Our ship will not cease leaking, else I think we had been halfway at Virginia. Our food will be half eaten up, I think, before we go from the coast of England.

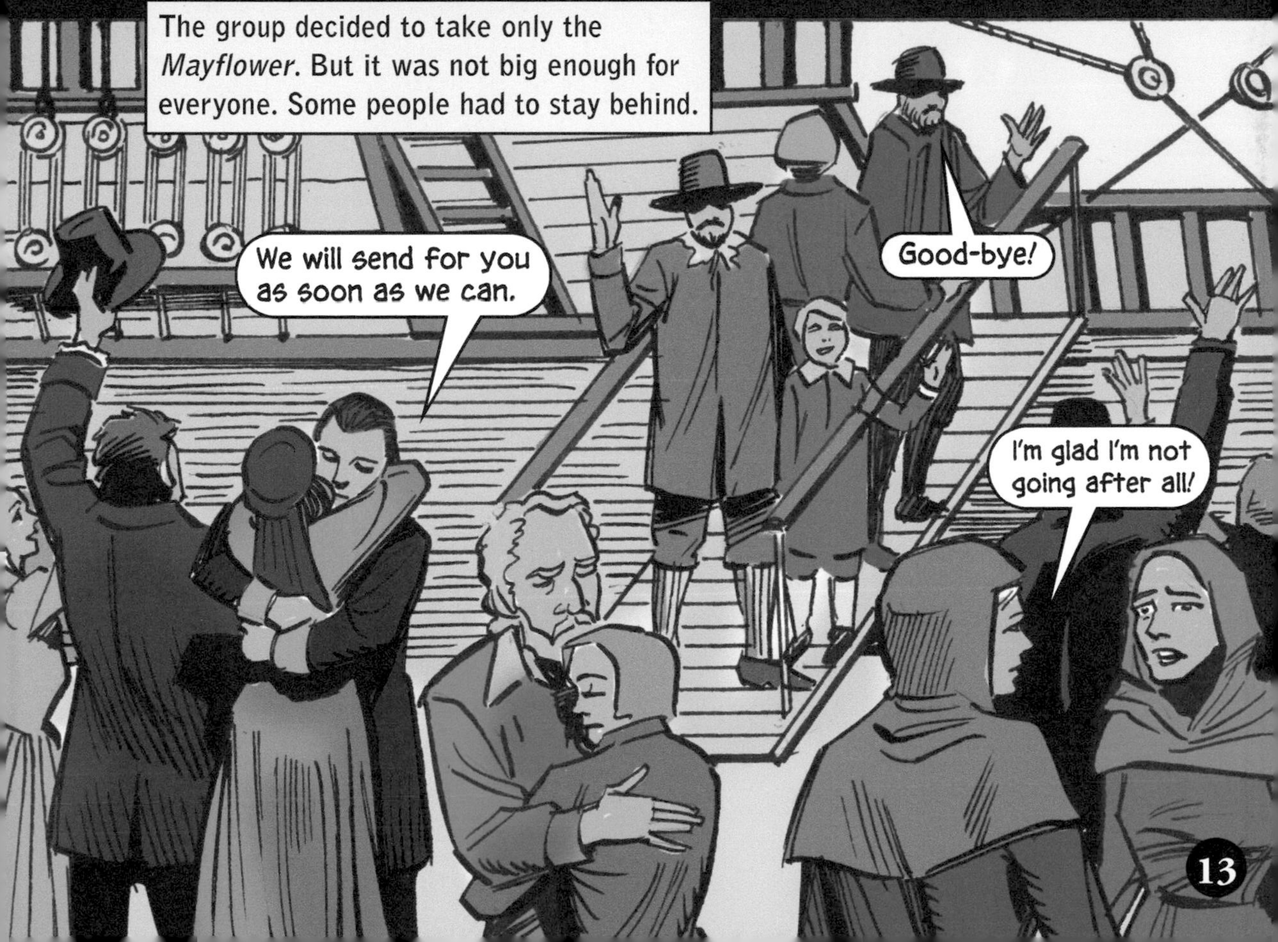
The group decided to take only the *Mayflower*. But it was not big enough for everyone. Some people had to stay behind.
We will send for you as soon as we can.
Good-bye!
I'm glad I'm not going after all!

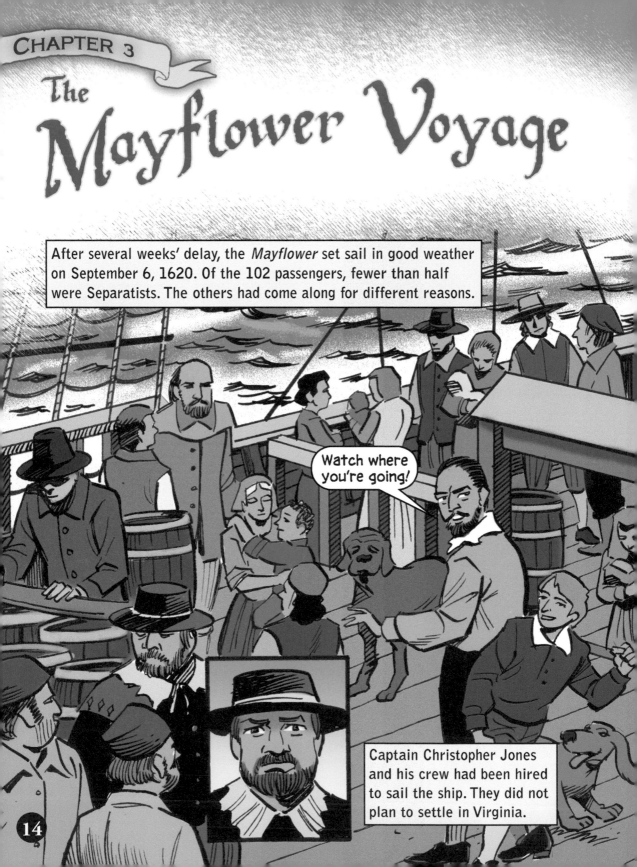

Chapter 3
The Mayflower Voyage

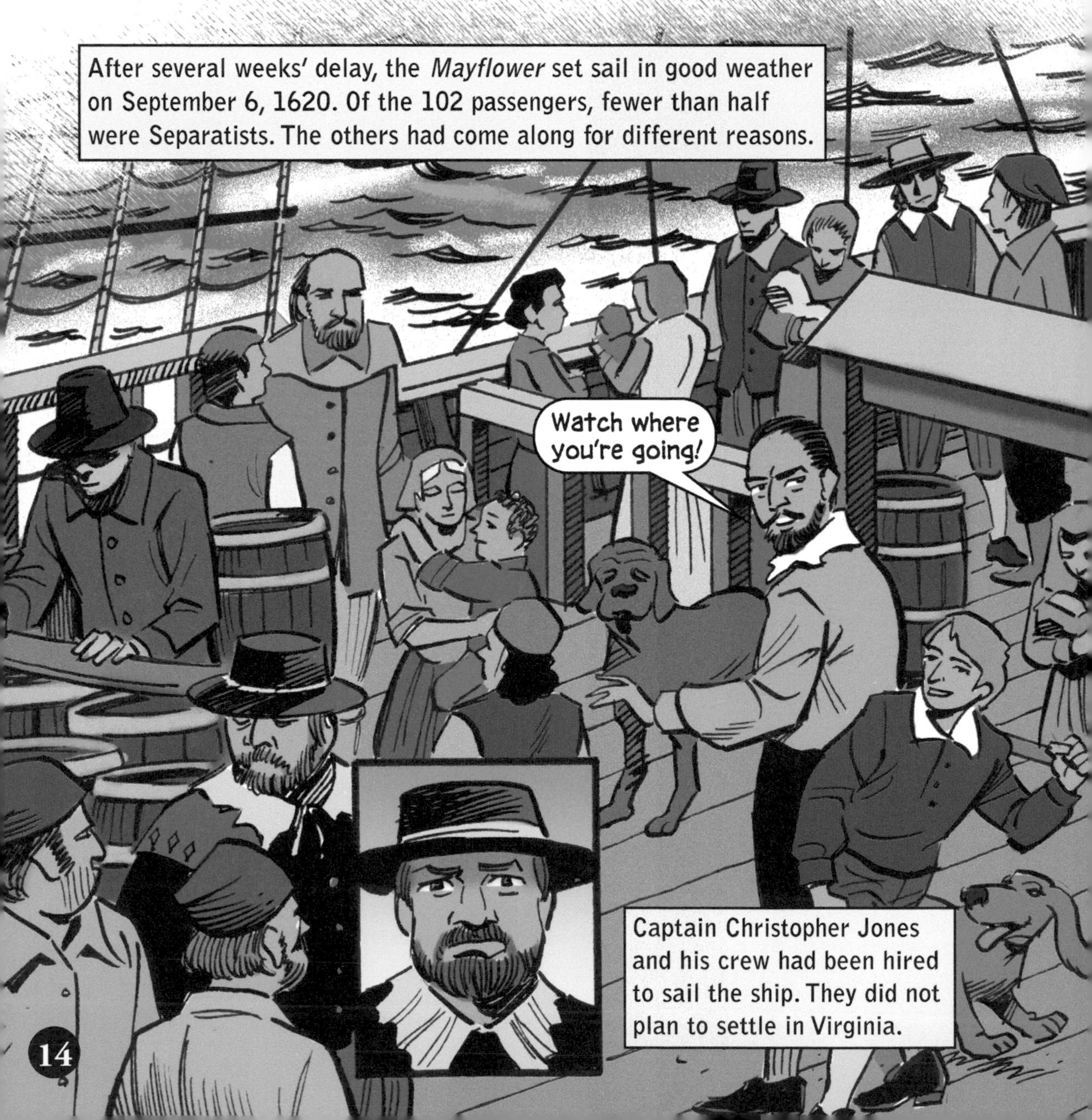

After several weeks' delay, the *Mayflower* set sail in good weather on September 6, 1620. Of the 102 passengers, fewer than half were Separatists. The others had come along for different reasons.
Watch where you're going!
Captain Christopher Jones and his crew had been hired to sail the ship. They did not plan to settle in Virginia.

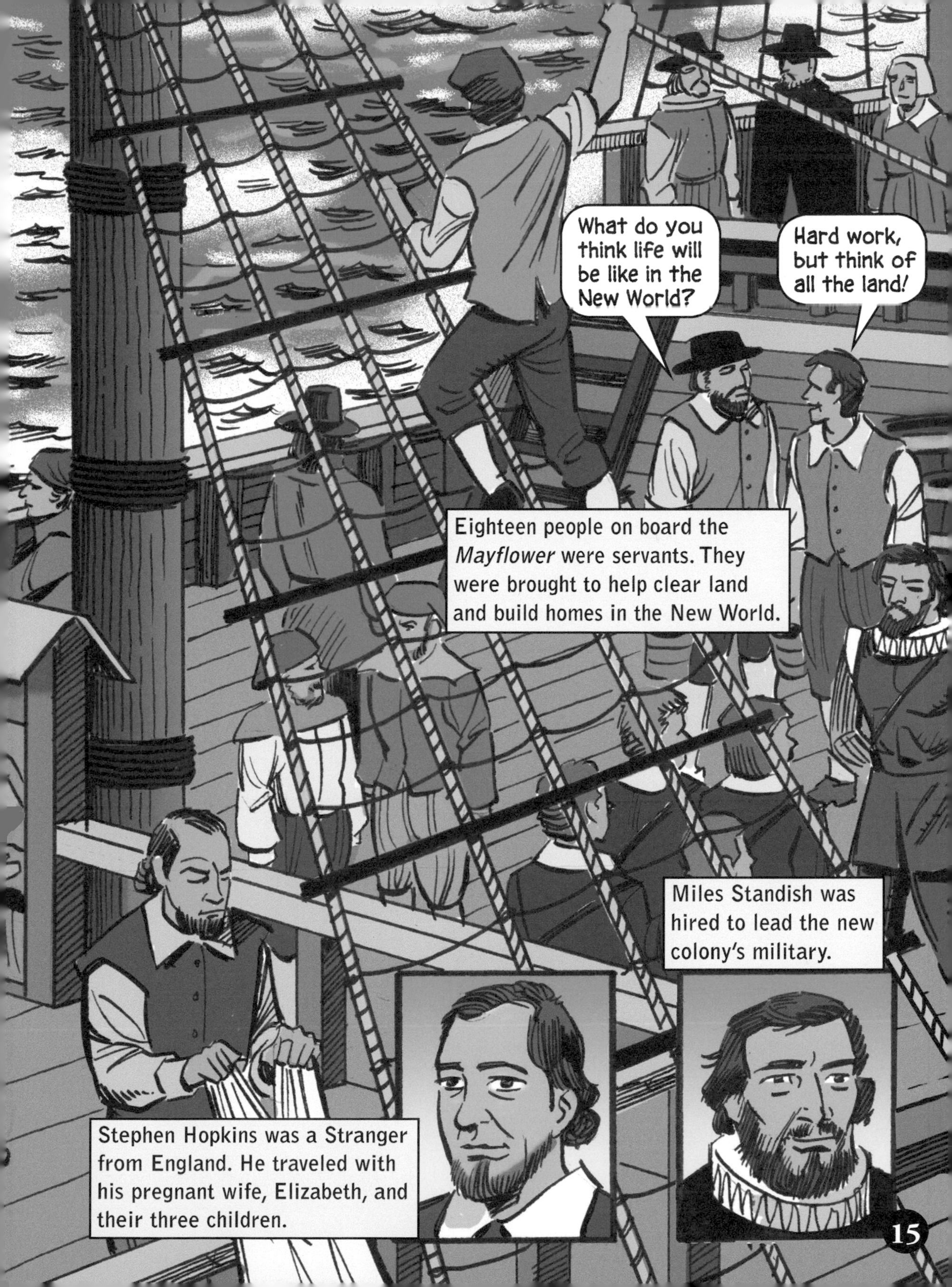
What do you think life will be like in the New World?
Hard work, but think of all the land!
Eighteen people on board the *Mayflower* were servants. They were brought to help clear land and build homes in the New World.
Miles Standish was hired to lead the new colony's military.
Stephen Hopkins was a Stranger from England. He traveled with his pregnant wife, Elizabeth, and their three children.

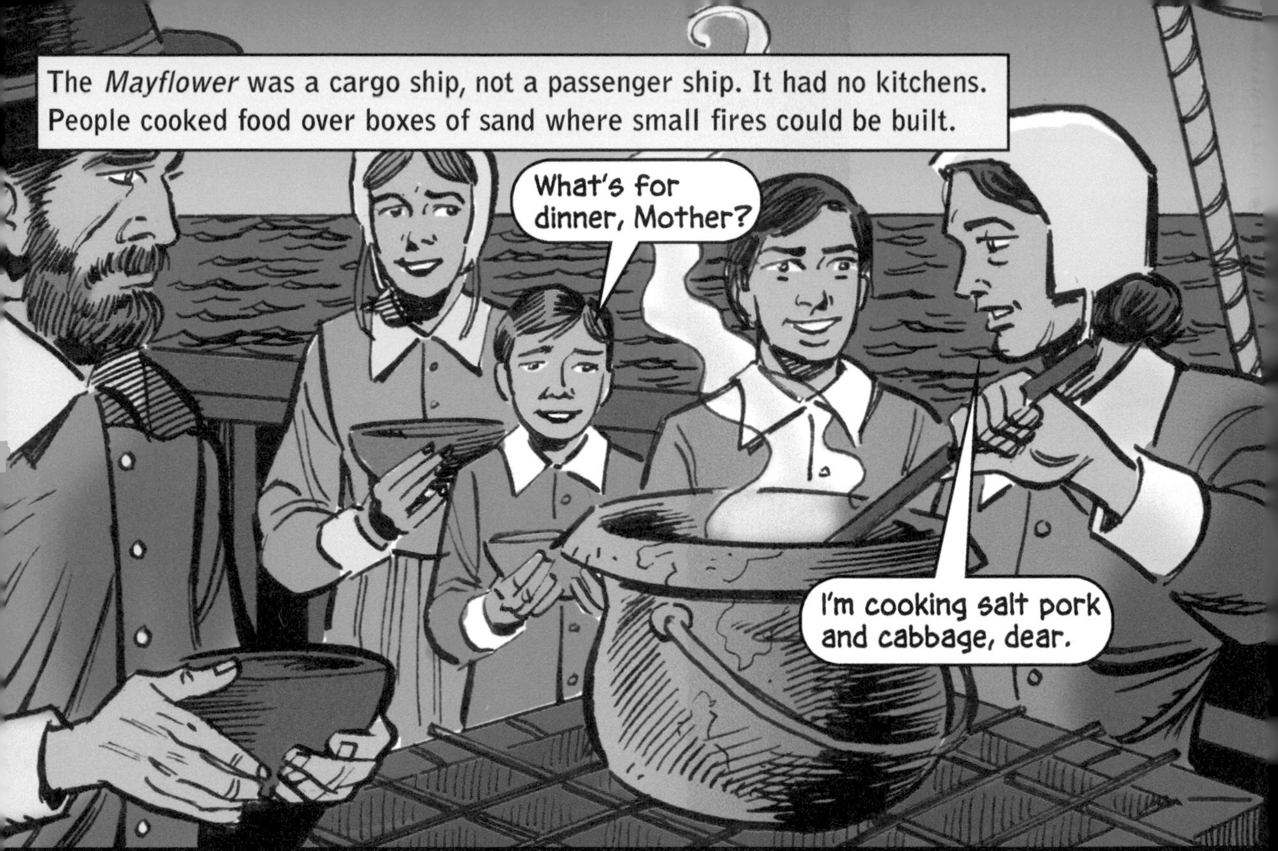
The Mayflower was a cargo ship, not a passenger ship. It had no kitchens. People cooked food over boxes of sand where small fires could be built.
What's for dinner, Mother?
I'm cooking salt pork and cabbage, dear.

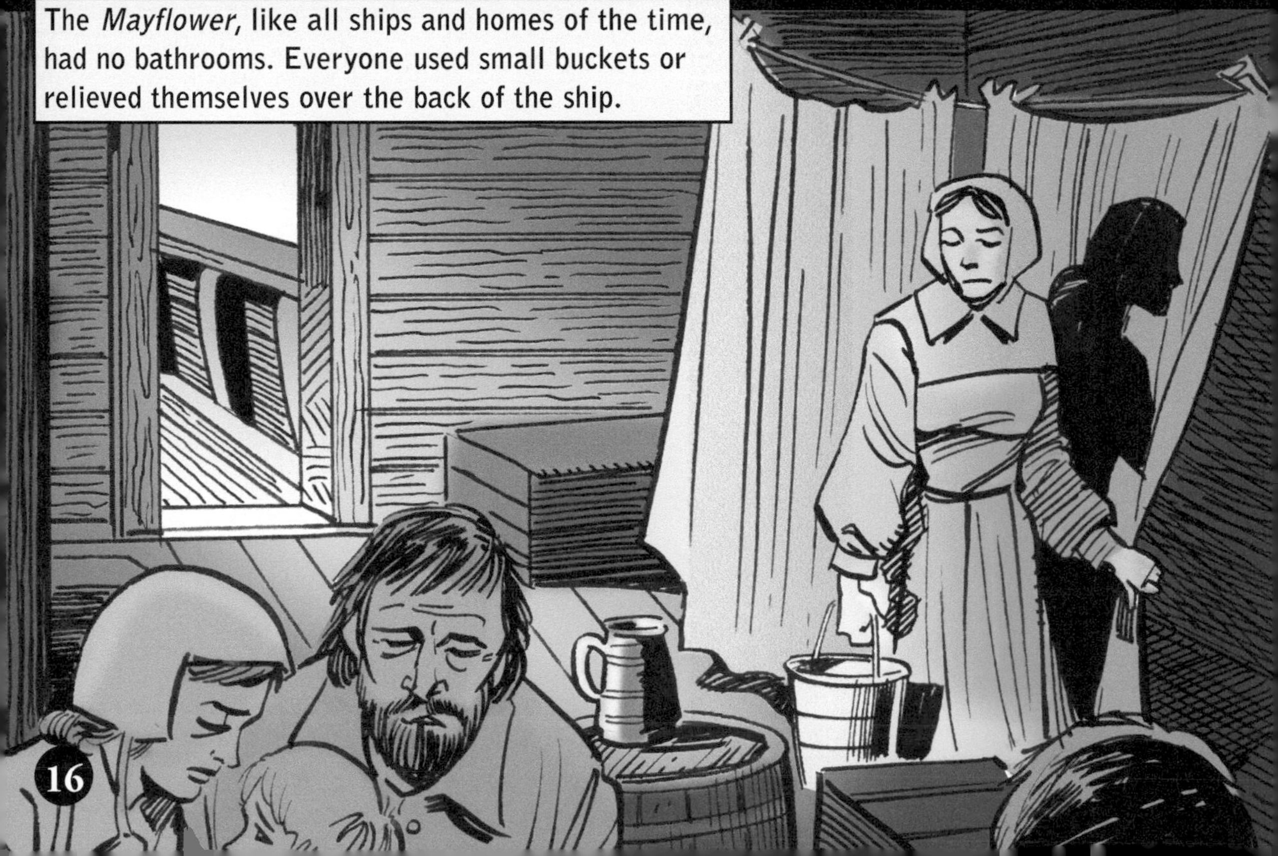
The Mayflower, like all ships and homes of the time, had no bathrooms. Everyone used small buckets or relieved themselves over the back of the ship.

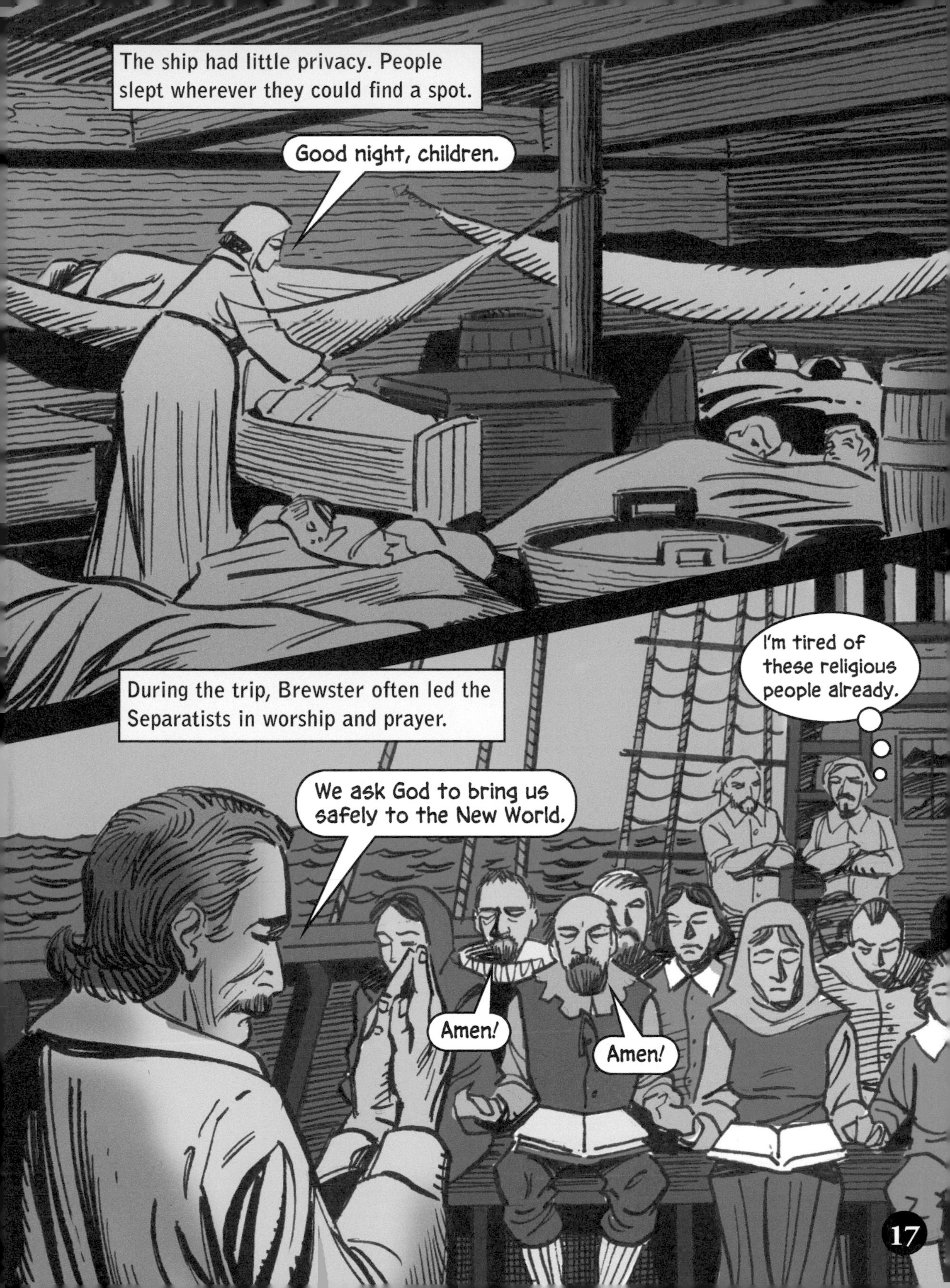
The ship had little privacy. People slept wherever they could find a spot.
Good night, children.
During the trip, Brewster often led the Separatists in worship and prayer.
We ask God to bring us safely to the New World.
Amen!
Amen!
I'm tired of these religious people already.

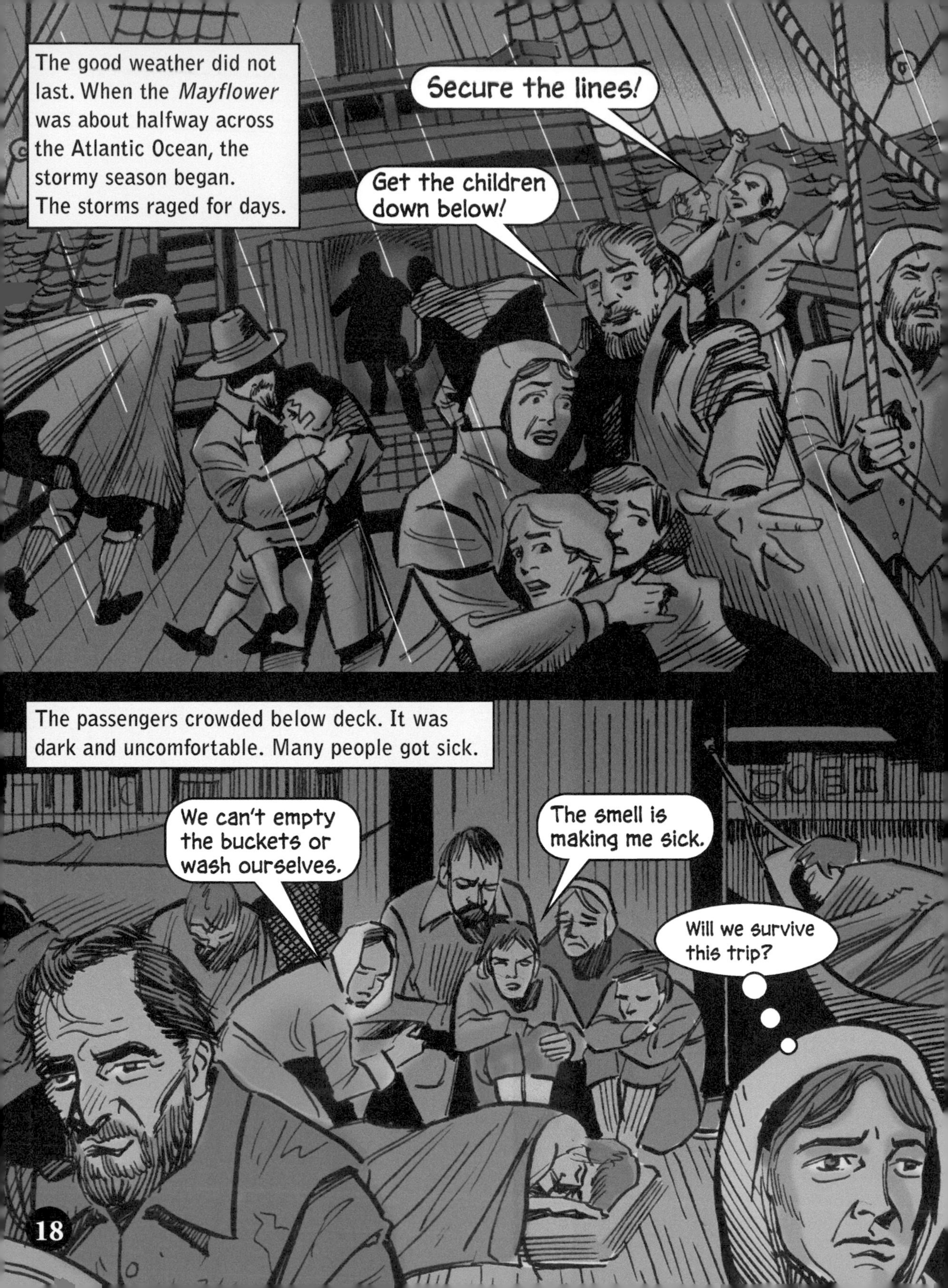
The good weather did not last. When the *Mayflower* was about halfway across the Atlantic Ocean, the stormy season began. The storms raged for days.
Secure the lines!
Get the children down below!
The passengers crowded below deck. It was dark and uncomfortable. Many people got sick.
We can't empty the buckets or wash ourselves.
The smell is making me sick.
Will we survive this trip?

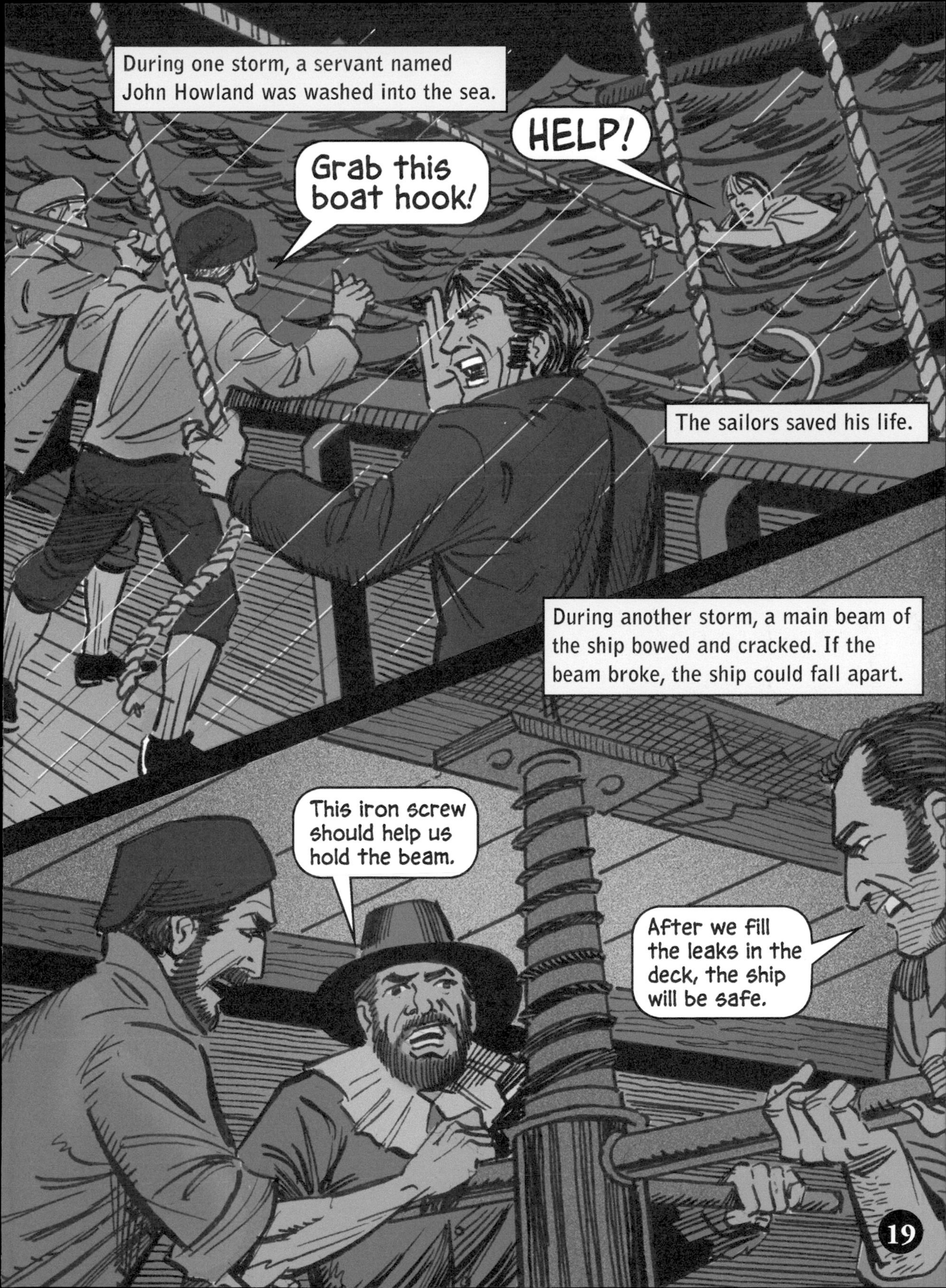
During one storm, a servant named John Howland was washed into the sea.
Grab this boat hook!
HELP!
The sailors saved his life.
During another storm, a main beam of the ship bowed and cracked. If the beam broke, the ship could fall apart.
This iron screw should help us hold the beam.
After we fill the leaks in the deck, the ship will be safe.

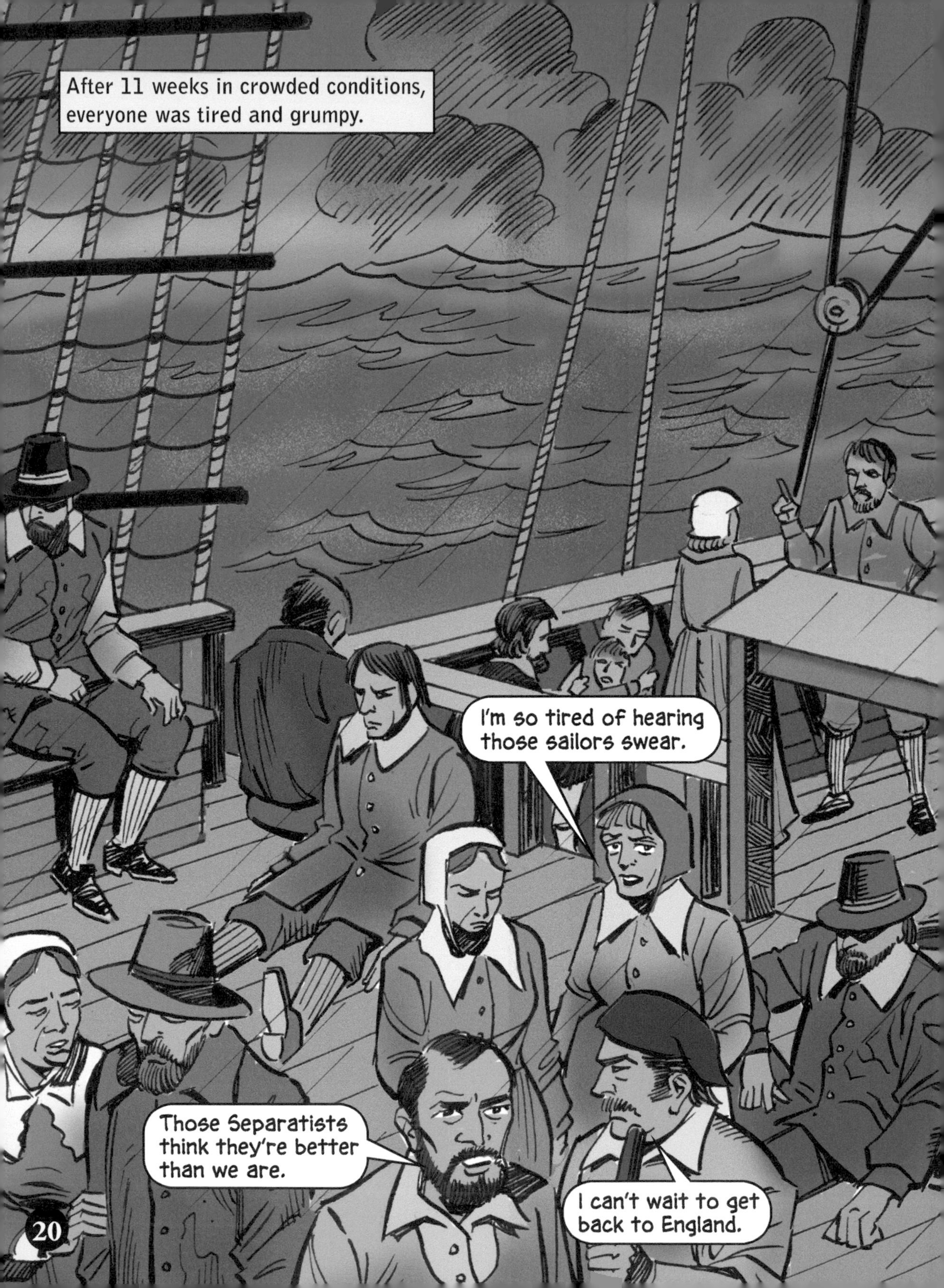
After 11 weeks in crowded conditions, everyone was tired and grumpy.
I'm so tired of hearing those sailors swear.
Those Separatists think they're better than we are.
I can't wait to get back to England.

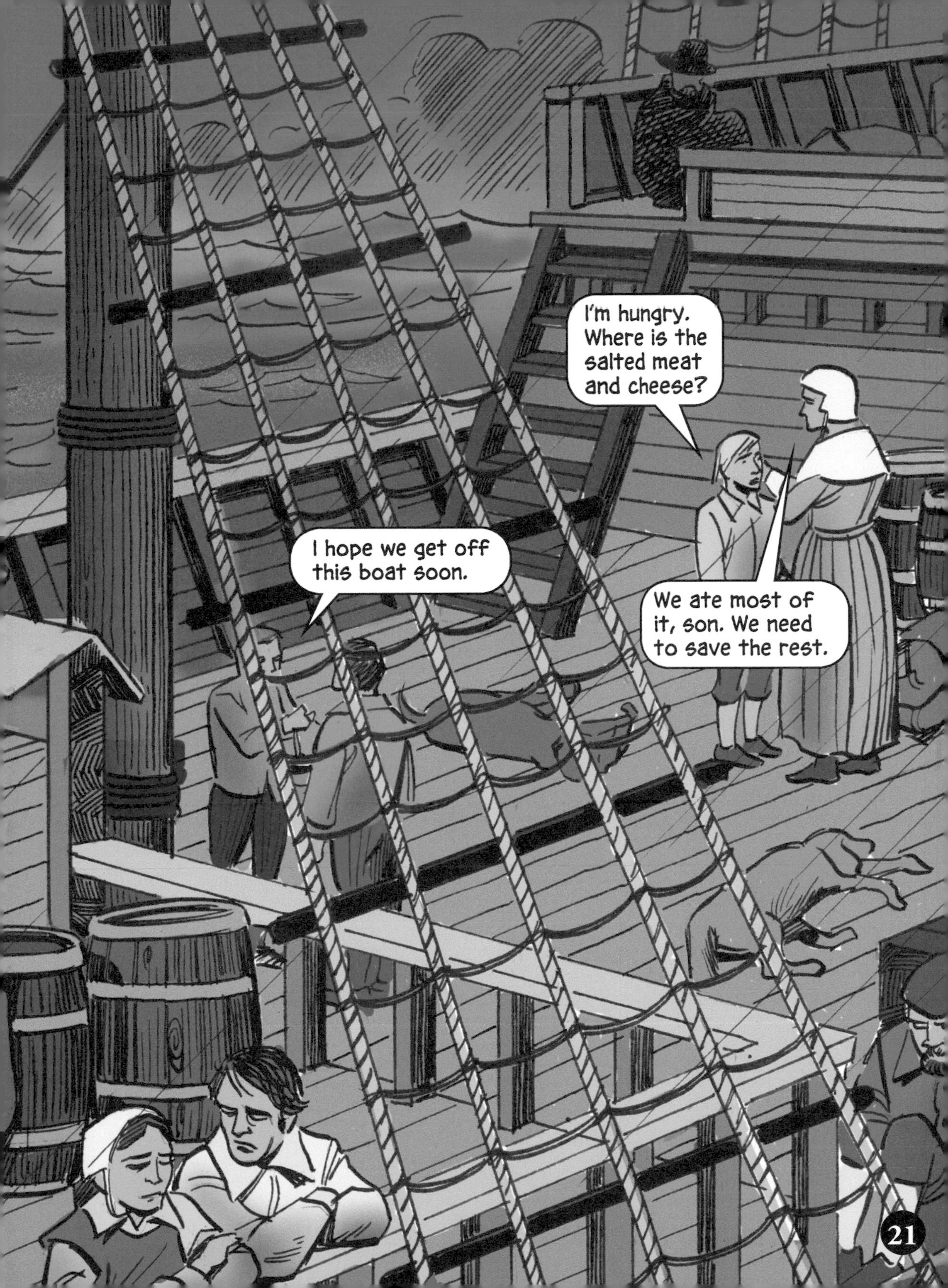
I'm hungry. Where is the salted meat and cheese?
We ate most of it, son. We need to save the rest.
I hope we get off this boat soon.

Chapter 4

The New World

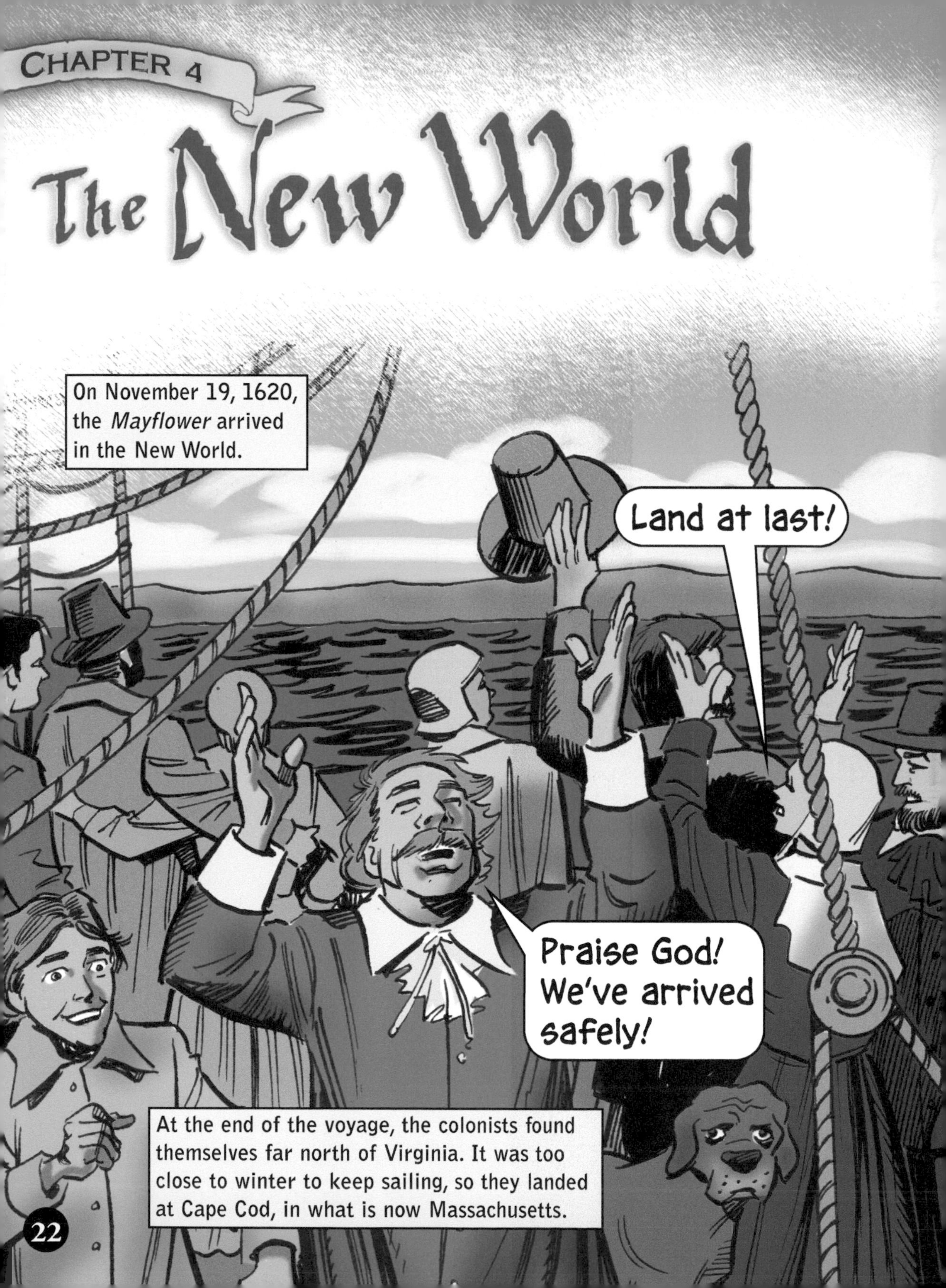

On November 19, 1620, the *Mayflower* arrived in the New World.
Land at last!
Praise God! We've arrived safely!
At the end of the voyage, the colonists found themselves far north of Virginia. It was too close to winter to keep sailing, so they landed at Cape Cod, in what is now Massachusetts.

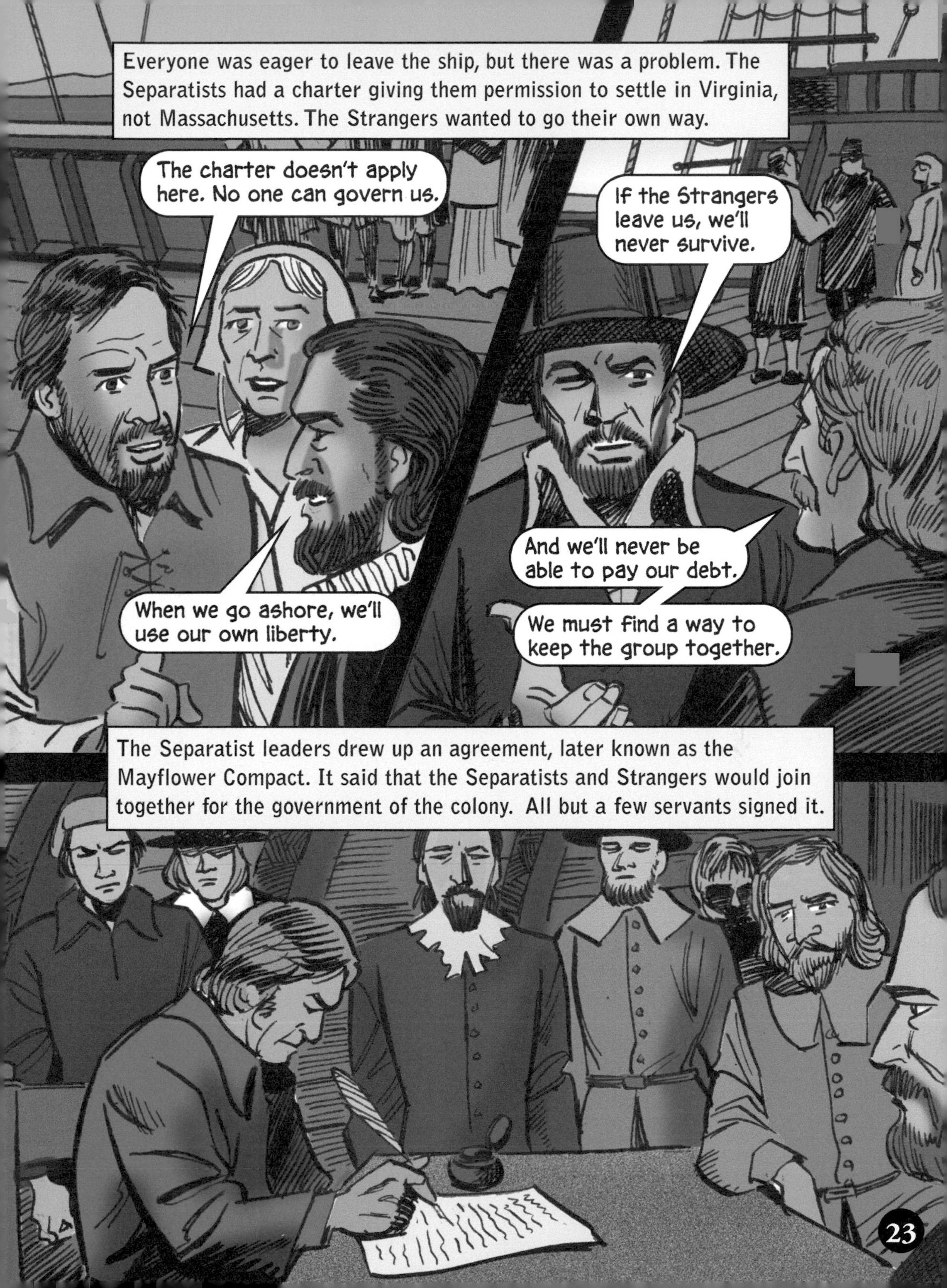
Everyone was eager to leave the ship, but there was a problem. The Separatists had a charter giving them permission to settle in Virginia, not Massachusetts. The Strangers wanted to go their own way.
The charter doesn't apply here. No one can govern us.
When we go ashore, we'll use our own liberty.
If the Strangers leave us, we'll never survive.
And we'll never be able to pay our debt.
We must find a way to keep the group together.
The Separatist leaders drew up an agreement, later known as the Mayflower Compact. It said that the Separatists and Strangers would join together for the government of the colony. All but a few servants signed it.

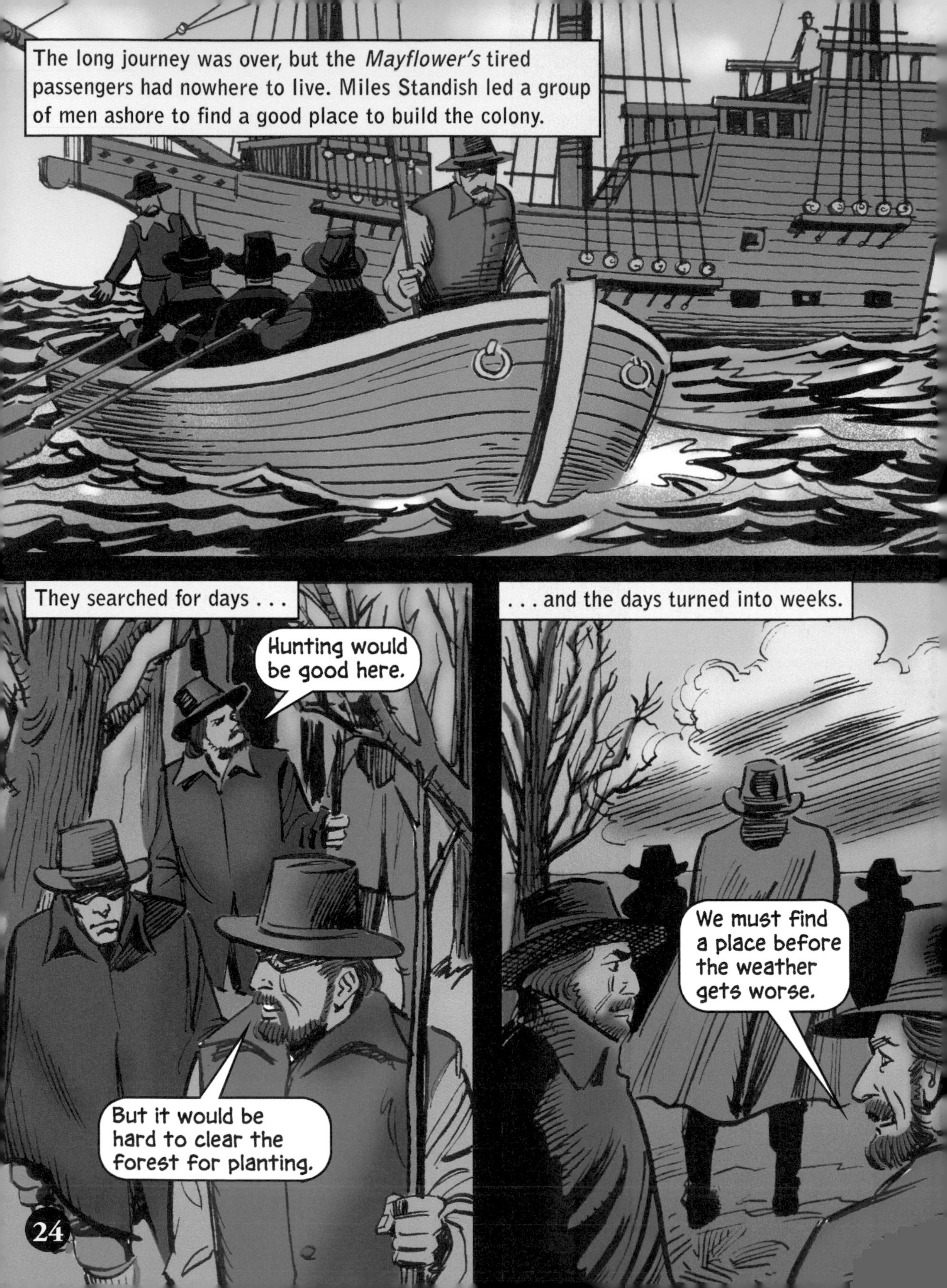
The long journey was over, but the *Mayflower's* tired passengers had nowhere to live. Miles Standish led a group of men ashore to find a good place to build the colony.
They searched for days . . .
Hunting would be good here.
But it would be hard to clear the forest for planting.
. . . and the days turned into weeks.
We must find a place before the weather gets worse.

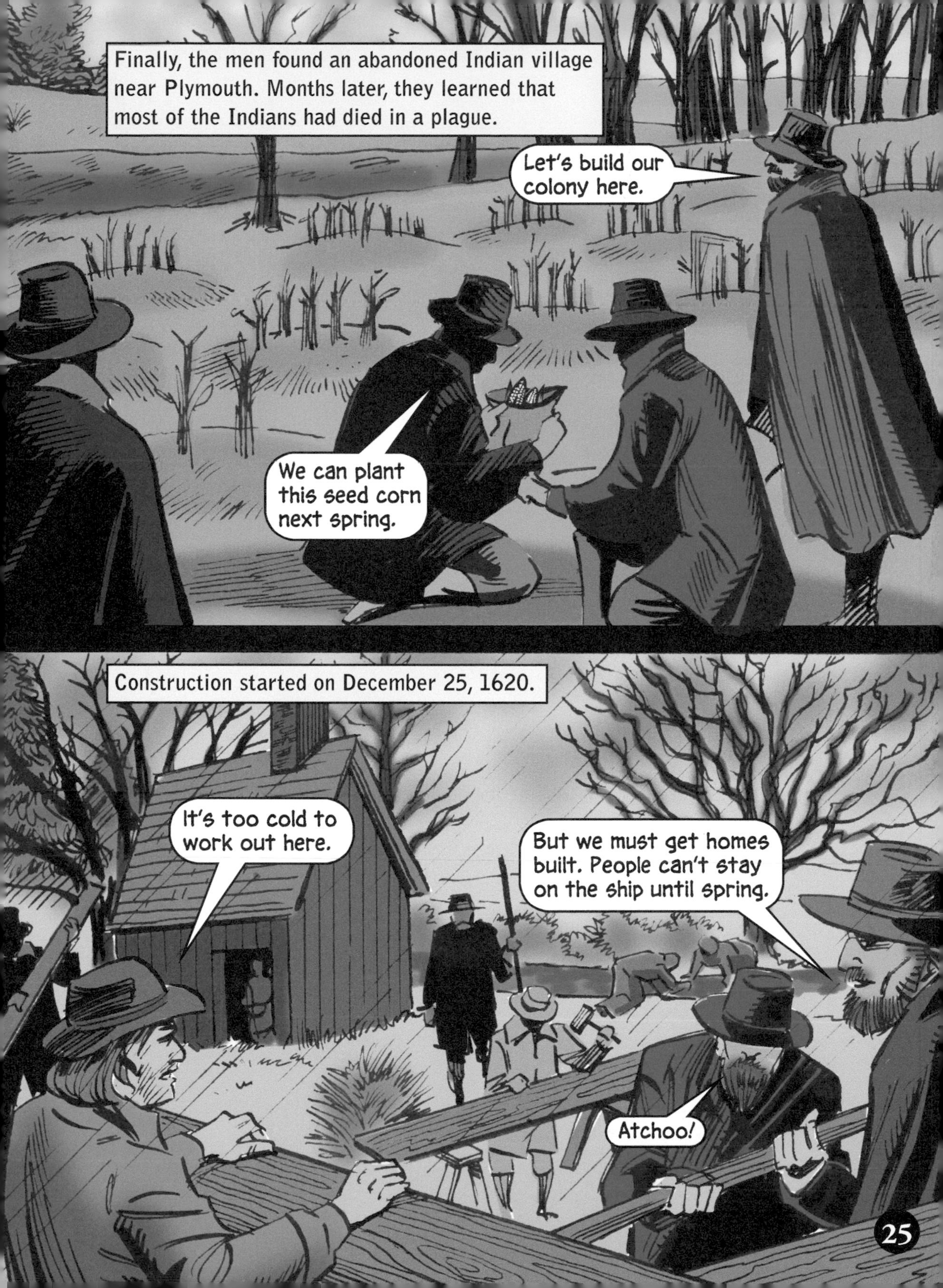
Finally, the men found an abandoned Indian village near Plymouth. Months later, they learned that most of the Indians had died in a plague.
Let's build our colony here.
We can plant this seed corn next spring.
Construction started on December 25, 1620.
It's too cold to work out here.
But we must get homes built. People can't stay on the ship until spring.
Atchoo!

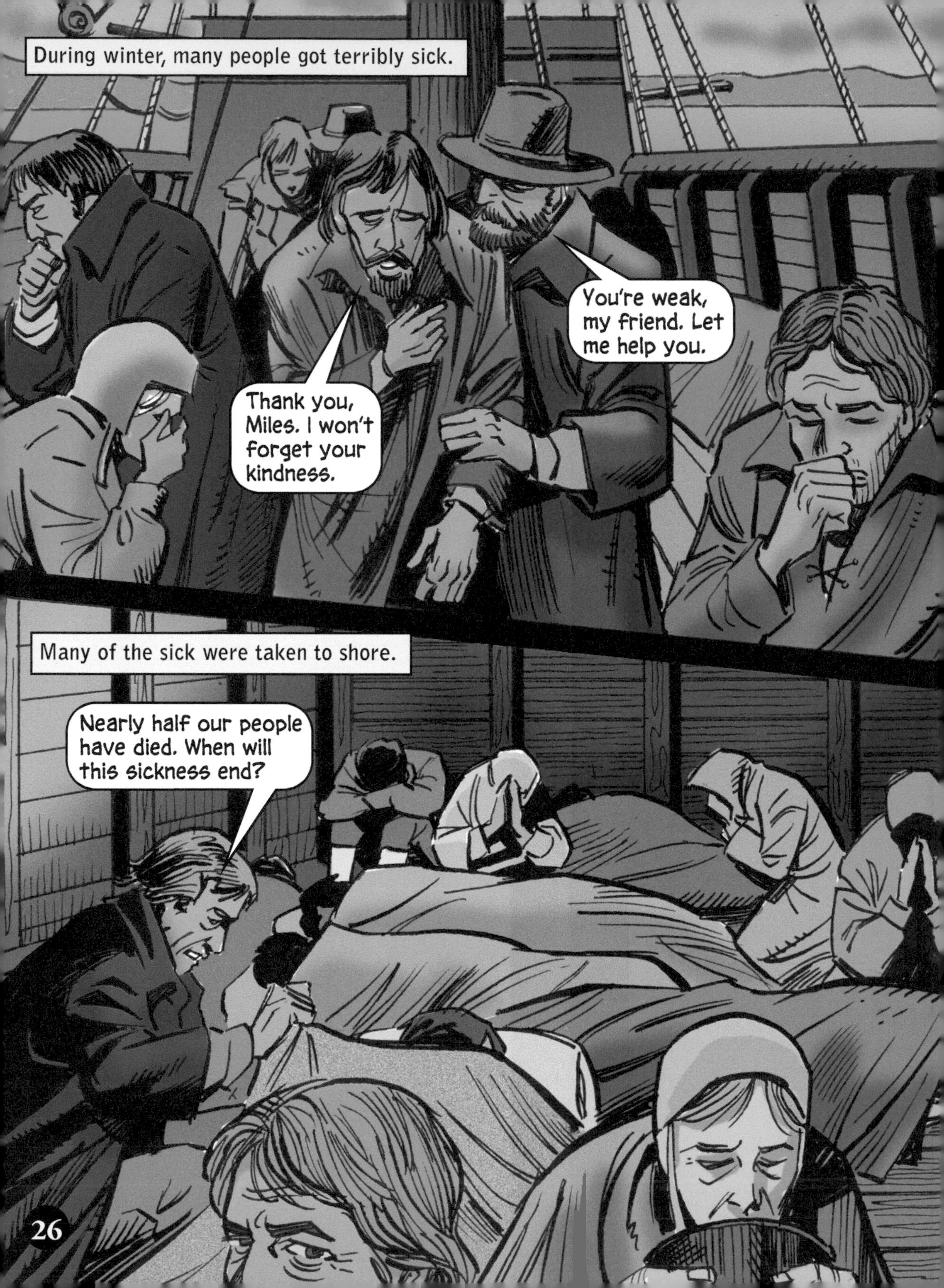
During winter, many people got terribly sick.
You're weak, my friend. Let me help you.
Thank you, Miles. I won't forget your kindness.
Many of the sick were taken to shore.
Nearly half our people have died. When will this sickness end?

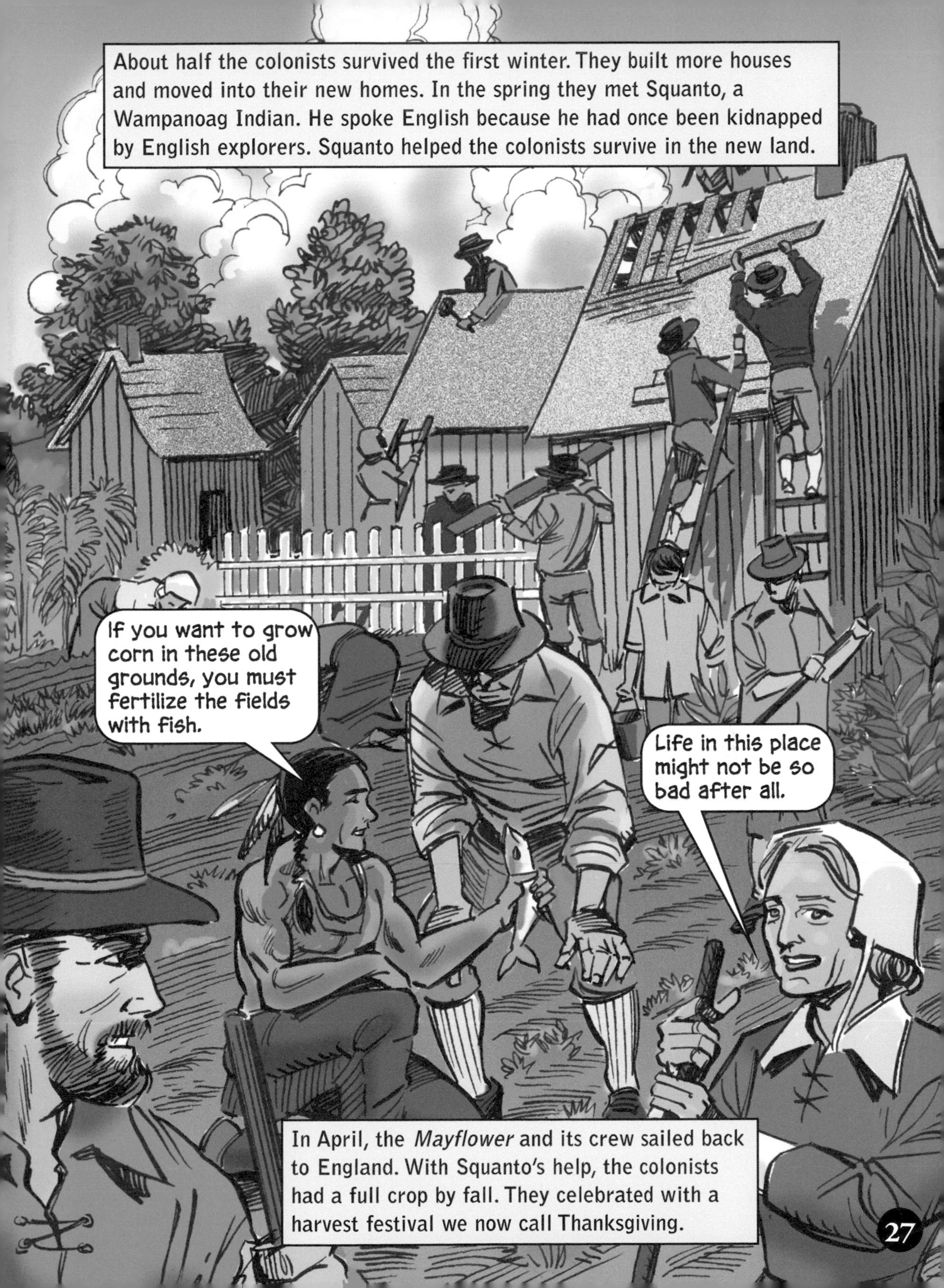
About half the colonists survived the first winter. They built more houses and moved into their new homes. In the spring they met Squanto, a Wampanoag Indian. He spoke English because he had once been kidnapped by English explorers. Squanto helped the colonists survive in the new land.
If you want to grow corn in these old grounds, you must fertilize the fields with fish.
Life in this place might not be so bad after all.
In April, the *Mayflower* and its crew sailed back to England. With Squanto's help, the colonists had a full crop by fall. They celebrated with a harvest festival we now call Thanksgiving.

More about the Mayflower

- The people on the *Mayflower* did not call themselves pilgrims. William Bradford first gave that name to the colonists in his book *Of Plymouth Plantation*. Bradford wrote this account during his lifetime, but it was not published until the 1800s.

- The *Mayflower* was built as a cargo ship. Before the ship transported people, it was used to carry wine and furs.

- The original *Mayflower* no longer exists. It is thought that parts of it were later used to build the roof of a barn in Buckinghamshire, England.

- William Mullins, a shoe and boot salesman, brought more than 250 shoes and 13 pairs of boots on the *Mayflower*. He hoped to sell them to the colonists.

- A young passenger named Francis Billington almost set the *Mayflower* on fire. He shot a musket inside a cabin near an open barrel of gunpowder.

During the voyage, Elizabeth Hopkins gave birth to a baby boy. She named him Oceanus because he was born on the ocean.

Many of the *Mayflower's* passengers got terribly seasick.

Only one person died while the *Mayflower* was at sea. He was a sailor who died from disease.

Passengers on the *Mayflower:*
  50 men
  19 women
  14 teenagers
  19 children

The average age of the men on the *Mayflower* was 34.

Glossary

cargo (KAR-goh)—freight that is carried by a ship

charter (CHAR-tur)—a document that gives a group the right to create a colony on a certain area of land and provides for a government

contract (KAHN-trakt)—a written agreement between two or more people or groups

elder (ELL-dur)—a leader of a religious group who is not a pastor or priest

invincible (in-VIN-suh-buhl)—incapable of being defeated

New World (NEW WURLD)—a term used by early colonists to refer to North America

plague (PLAYG)—a serious disease that spreads quickly to many people and often causes death

sabotage (SA-buh-tahzh)—to purposely destroy property to stop an activity

Internet Sites

FactHound offers a safe, fun way to find Internet sites related to this book. All of the sites on FactHound have been researched by our staff.

Here's how:

1. *Visit www.facthound.com*
2. Type in this special code **073684371X** for age-appropriate sites. Or enter a search word related to this book for a more general search.
3. Click on the **Fetch It** button.

FactHound will fetch the best sites for you!

Read More

Apel, Melanie Ann. *The Pilgrims.* Daily Life. San Diego: KidHaven Press, 2003.

Brooks, Phillip. *The Mayflower Compact.* We the People. Minneapolis: Compass Point Books, 2005.

Dell, Pamela. *The Plymouth Colony.* Let Freedom Ring. Mankato, Minn.: Capstone Press, 2004.

Hirschfelder, Arlene B. *Squanto: 1585?–1622.* American Indian Biographies. Mankato, Minn.: Blue Earth Books, 2004.

Plimoth Plantation. *Mayflower 1620: A New Look at a Pilgrim Voyage.* Washington, D.C.: National Geographic, 2003.

Bibiliography

Bradford, William. *Of Plymouth Plantation.* New York: Alfred Knopf, 1952.

Caffrey, Kate. *The Mayflower.* New York: Stein and Day, 1974.

Deetz, James, and Patricia Scott Deetz. *The Times of Their Lives: Life, Love, and Death in Plymouth Colony.* New York: W.H. Freeman, 2000.

Dillon, Francis. *The Pilgrims.* Garden City, N. Y.: Doubleday, 1975.

Mourt, G. *Mourt's Relation: A Journal of the Pilgrims at Plymouth.* New York: Corinth Books, 1963.

Index